BRITAIN IN OLD PHOTOGRAPHS

SANDOWN &
SHANKLIN

DONALD A. PARR

SUTTON PUBLISHING LIMITED

Sutton Publishing Limited
Phoenix Mill · Far Thrupp · Stroud
Gloucestershire · GL5 2BU

First published 1996

Title page: Sandown Carnegie Free Library in
the High Street, 1935, proudly flying the Union
Jack. Over decades the library has undergone
many changes, including the formation of a
geological museum which houses a small but
informative collection of dinosaur remains.

British Library Cataloguing in Publication Data
A catalogue record for this book is available from the
British Library.

ISBN 0-7509-1131-X

Typeset in 10/12 Perpetua.
Typesetting and origination by
Sutton Publishing Limited.
Printed in Great Britain by
Ebenezer Baylis, Worcester.

One of the worst snowstorms ever recorded on the Isle of Wight was in 1881. Featured is George
Merman's, grocer, tea dealer and house agent, but with the amount of snow which had fallen during the
night, it was not 'business as usual'.

CONTENTS

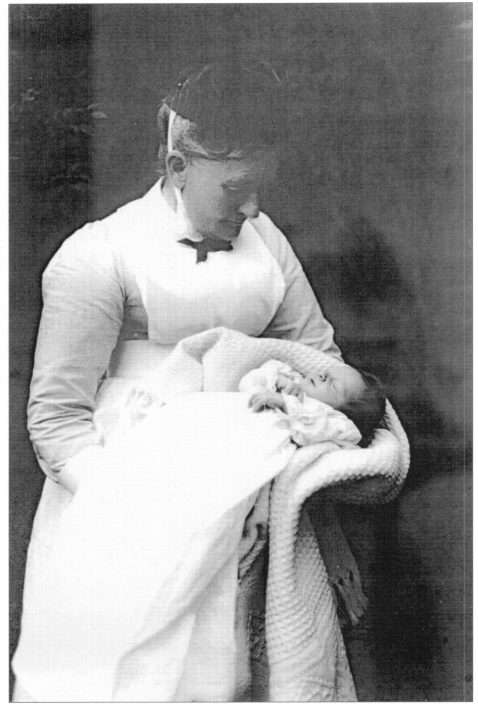

This picture, probably taken in the early 1900s, shows Nurse Bull with one of those she helped into this world. It is said that Nurse Bull would go to the confinement on an old tricycle.

Mrs Hendy's school concert at Elswick House, Station Avenue, Sandown, in the early 1900s. The Scottish boy, Edgar Thomas, became one of the well-known longshoremen of Sandown. The little girl dressed as a Welsh lady, on the far right, is Evelyn Higgs, a well-known member of the Baptist Church, who will always be remembered for her kindness.

INTRODUCTION

In this, the fifth book of the series, I feel I owe no apology for 'twinning' these two towns, for many holidays in my youth were spent either in Sandown or Shanklin. They are just as popular today as they were then, as are the surrounding villages such as Alverstone, Apse Heath, Arreton, Brading, Lake, Newchurch and St Helens, to quote just a few examples mentioned in this book.

I often, therefore, regard it as a little strange that neither Sandown or Shanklin enjoyed popularity with tourists until the late 1800s, and because of this it will be necessary in this introduction to separate these near identical twins for just a short while before uniting them again when we return to modern times.

Sandown in the 1850s was virtually non-existent as a residential area, having well under a hundred houses. I often feel that we would know a little more about it had a writer, who in the 1780s left a legacy of stories about the island, had taken the trouble to speak to the few good folk who lived there, but he simply described Sandown as 'a village by a sandy shore'.

A small piece of recorded history – although not completely substantiated – concerns John Wilkes, Member of Parliament. Towards the end of his life this playboy of his day made Sandown his home, where he led an eccentric existence. His money, life style and dazzling suits of scarlet trimmed with gold rather turned the heads of the young girls; thus it is said that he sired many illegitimate offspring, and cooled his wine in a memorial imitation of Virgil's tomb which he had made in memory of a poet friend. Whether this is all true or not is subject to speculation, but he was regarded as a pretty useless MP. His one saving grace was probably that in 1790 he was responsible and saw through the bill for freedom from arbitrary arrest. Should the above information be true, then maybe he had himself in mind!

I would have thought that someone, somewhere would have recorded for posterity something about this lovely resort, but as far as I know no one ever did, so bygone Sandown slipped through the net until comparatively modern times when local historians have commenced piecing together the past days of this idyllic spot.

Shanklin has slightly more of an historic past. In the 1870s there were 355 recorded residents, 255 more than the population in 1790, but it still only covered the area of present-day Shanklin Old Village and once again very little has been known about it until quite recently.

Absolutely substantiated is the fact that in 1880 French poet Paul Bourget came to live in Shanklin and described it as picturesque, prosperous and respectable, 'a classical village of romance with lawns and pretty cottages covered with rambling roses'. However, he also regarded Shanklin as an extremely solemn place, especially on Sunday when the shops would all close, no intoxicating liqueur was served anywhere and everyone proceeded to one of the four churches.

In these days of tourism, when both towns have spread considerably with populations exceeding 40,000 residents and anything up to 600,000 visitors in the summer, I often wonder how people could have been melancholy in such a happy area, with the clean sweeps of beaches and waves chasing each other as if to be first home in the race and everyone appearing to enjoy themselves. Were the children allowed much time for play with their buckets and spades? Apparently, children's fun was also curtailed very carefully, reflecting the unenlightened and more than a little sanctimonious attitude which pervaded that era.

Sandown and Shanklin are now two of the prime island tourist spots. Sandown pier theatre is famous for good summer shows and visits by well-known stars who appear on Sunday evenings. Shanklin, too, boasts a good theatre and until the hurricanes of October 1987 also possessed a popular pier. In one night the structure was destroyed and pieces of the 100-year-old pier, including metal stanchions, were twisted and flung across the beach like matchwood. Maybe one day someone will take it into his head to do something about rebuilding it, but we will have to wait. The island wheels turn slowly but invariably get there in the end.

This applies to the whole island, even to these two crowded south coast resorts, for, in spite of the happy joyous crowds and the numerous hotels, guest houses, restaurants, amusement arcades, sports facilities, a famous zoo and many other tourist attractions, the slow pace, which has changed very little in over two hundred years, is still a welcome change to the hustle and bustle of life on the mainland.

The area has little in common with Newport, Ryde, Cowes and East Cowes or Ventnor and District as featured in the other island books in this series. It is in fact very little akin to any other area. This is why a great many families return to Sandown and Shanklin year after year. They are made welcome, prices are reasonable and the majority of people, residents and visitors alike, always seem to be happy.

Donald A. Parr, 1996

THE PEOPLE

Even in 1924 Shanklin railway station was not a place for a fashion show, unless your name happened to be Dora Lodder, who is pictured showing off her new Sunday dress.

Ladder making is one village craft which unfortunately seems to have died out. In this photograph, *c*. 1890, Mr Mackett is in his garden workshop at Newchurch.

A day out from Eastney in Hampshire to the Isle of Wight in 1921 — quite a treat. Young Olive Stone, her mother and grandmother are among this group watching a Punch and Judy show on the beach at Shanklin.

The village thatcher is almost a thing of the past, but here we see Vic Hiscock, thatcher at Newchurch, plying his trade in 1950.

In 1925, when this picture was taken, Drabbles Estate of Sandown had many gardeners. Among those pictured are Mr Niblett and Mr Draper (Head Gardeners), Mr Cassford, Mr Shave and Mr White, who was killed during the First World War.

During the Second World War, those who were not called to arms for any reason did their part. Pictured here in his ARP uniform, Will Jacobs was no exception.

Officers of the 'Pleasant Sunday Afternoon Club', a brotherhood who met at the Congregational Church in Leed Street, Sandown. Pictured here are (left to right) Bruce Denness, P. Marewood Corney, a police officer and Mr Butcher. They are returning with a police escort from the bank in the early 1900s with cash for the annual slate share-out of savings prior to the Christmas distribution.

Sandown 'Pleasant Sunday Afternoon Club', date unknown. From left to right: Messrs P.H. Compton, P. Marewood Corney, Butcher, Revd D.M. Bynner, the local police officer, -?- and Bruce Denness..

Mr and Mrs Bull, 1890. Mrs Bull was well known as the local midwife for the Alverstone and Sandown District.

Nurse Bull in a garden adjacent to the old gasworks in Sandown, now the offices for the South Wight Housing Association. Nurse Bull died in 1935.

Clarks (IOW) annual outing, believed to be to Blenheim Palace, in the early 1960s. Included are Graham Ford, Miss Duff, Gwen Weston, Dawn Rook, Norah Green, Eileen Clark, Eric Weston, Bill Clark (The Boss), Mrs Eldridge, Mr Rice, Ruth Lucas, Mr Gilbert, Jim Eldridge, Mr Smith, Mrs Dyer, Mr Weeks, Mr Child, Les Lucas, Norman Jeffries, Mr Green, Evan Jolliffe, Ernie Duff, Reg Millward, Mr Dyer, Betty Millward, Barbara Jolliffe, Tom Chiverton and Sue Caldwell.

This photograph remains an enigma, not only to ourselves but also to its owners, the Sandown Civic Archives. It is believed to have been taken outside the Baptist Church, date unknown, and features Mr W. Young and Mr F. Walker. If anyone has further information please contact Terry Hall at Sandown Civic Centre.

Sandown General School teachers in July 1920. Included are Mr J.B. Irving, Mr H.J. Hooper, Mr C.W. Turner, Miss C. Bevan, Miss Buller, Mr Parnell and Dr J.H. Parkinson.

Mr Tullidge, the shepherd at Manor Farm, Shanklin, prior to the White-Pophams owning the estate. This picture was taken in about 1870.

Henry Brown, fisherman of Sandown, 1915. Henry also had a shop in Melville Street which sold wet fish and poultry. Whenever conversation was started with him, he would always launch into the story about the time a crab bit his toe.

Members of Sandown Royal British Legion pose for a group photograph outside the Rivoli Cinema after visiting the newly opened picture house in 1921. At the time this was a novelty to exceed all novelties.

The opening of the canoe lake at Sandown in 1930. Pictured here are Messrs Thompson, Harmon, Broad, Findon, Dutton, R. Hooper, I. Hooper and Mrs H. de Vere Stockpool.

This is believed to be Mrs White-Popham taking in the sea air at Sandown, 1899.

Sandown firemen aboard the Lymington–Yarmouth ferry in 1923. Mr W.N. Brown, Ernest Dyer (with pipe) and Stan Woodnutt (standing at back) had been taking part in the Southern District Competition Drills.

'Blackey' Scovell and his son Harry pose by their workshop at Sandown. The date is unknown.

Francis White-Popham, last Lord of the Manor at Shanklin, who was born in 1829 and died in 1894.

Mrs White-Popham, Lady of the Manor at Shanklin until her death in 1929.

Mr Bailey, the bailiff to the Lord of the Manor, Francis White-Popham, 1892.

Elizabeth Daish (née Winter), 1870. She was born in 1779 and died at the ripe old age of ninety-eight. Elizabeth had twelve children, one of whom was Jack, who later founded Daish's Hotel.

Even in 1920, MPs were called upon to perform many functions outside Parliament. Sir Edgar Chatfield-Clark MP is pictured opening a fête and floral show at Newchurch.

Mr Kemp, known to all as 'Diddler', was a fisherman and longshoreman in Sandown at the turn of the century.

'Diddler' again, this time with his bag of lobsters.

Mr Blake, longshoreman, on the beach at Sandown. This photograph was probably taken in the 1930s.

SPORT

This certificate of the Isle of Wight County Bowling Association for the League Championship Division 2 was won by Shanklin Bowling Club in 1960.

The Football Club at Lake Park in 1909. Among those pictured are Alan Goring, Len Pearce, Mr Henderson, George Keil, Bert Denham, Fred Woods, Mr King, Gordon Locke, Will Arnold and Jack Owen.

Sandown Schoolboys Football Team in the 1951–2 season. Back row, left to right: Ray (Tich) Pardey, -?-, Jim Walters, David Stillwell, Hugh Lane, Brian Sheath, Mr Robin Marshall. Front row: -?-, Alex Woodhouse, Colin Bastiani, Richard Saunders, -?-.

Sandown Football Club in 1934–5. Among those pictured are L. George James, D. Berry, Alan Gray, Charlie Butler, Charlie Betts, Alf Kieling, Reg Taylor, Sid Carpenter and Mr Jeffries.

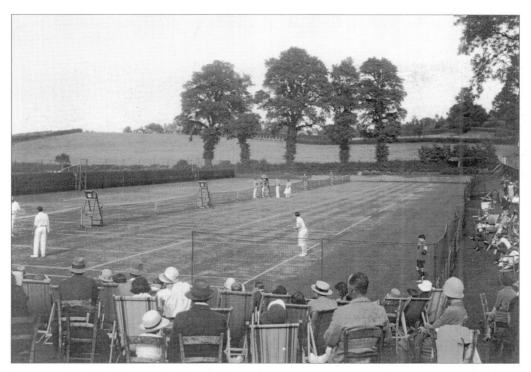

At one time Drabbles Estate in Sandown held annual tennis competitions on their own courts which were situated in an area now occupied by 'The Heights' leisure centre. This picture is thought to have been taken in the mid-1920s.

The smiling faces of the boys of Newchurch County Primary School tell it all. A small school team take on all opponents and still come out the winners, but their motto was 'Smile when you play not just when you win'. Included in this photograph of 1920 are Edward Groves, Edgar Taylor, William Taylor, Fred Harvey, William Groves and Harold Taylor.

Brown's Golf Course, Sandown, 1936. Many holiday-makers will remember the fun of the putting green, and the added pleasure of Brown's famous doughnuts.

In the 1930s, before the advent of piped home entertainment, people would go out more into the countryside and make their own amusement. Here on Arreton Down on 21 July 1935 is the start of a slow bicycle race, the winner being the last to reach the tape. One rule only: feet must not leave the pedals!

The Sandown Wednesday football team, 1935/6 season. Back row, left to right: John Meguyer, Bern Rush, Clive Heslam, Wilf Brett, Ray Lewis, Arthur Meguyer, -?-, Ted Tremear. Front row: Ray Clark, Ted Lewis, ? MacGonnel, -?-, Frank Theakston, John Healy.

Sandown Golf Course, 1927. The greens have altered little since this photograph was taken by Mr R. Woodnutt.

These two photographs show Sandown Schoolgirls hockey teams in 1920, the 1st Eleven (above) and the 2nd Eleven (below). In the picture below, back row, second from left is Kate Mew, who was later known for her pork pie shop at the bottom of the High Street. She also became one of the governors of Sandown Grammar School.

Shanklin Wednesday football team, 1913/14 season. Back row, left to right: W. Salter, R. Howard, W. Matthews, ? Lardner. Middle row: -?-, S. Hatcher, S. Percival, ? Stamp, -?-. Front row: -?-, 'Babe' Simmonds, -?-.

Apse Heath football team, 1936. Back row, left to right: Guy, Sibbick, Driver. Middle row: Young, Stallard, McDonald. Front row: Holbrook, Mew, Whitlock, Brown, Whittington.

Apse Heath Social Club with four trophies. Back row, left to right: Denness, Hargreaves, Smith, Groves, Sibbick, Lavers. Front row: Tibbles, Morris, Guy, Barton, Steward.

Newchurch football team, 1946/7 season. Back row, left to right: Bravery, Lavers, Francis. Middle row: Taylor, Moody, Stallard. Front row: Hayden, Russell, Austin, Hargreaves, Stephens.

Shanklin Youth Club football team, league winners 1947. Back row, left to right: T. Bevis, D. Dallimore, J. Martin, D. Cameron, L. Martin, J. Clarkson. Front row: P. Gibbon, D. Gallop, C. Groves, D.Newnham, N. Rann. The mascot is Jack Martin's youngest brother.

Shanklin Wednesday football team, 1925. Back row, left to right: Mr Jefferies, Mr Jefferies, Mr Perkins, F. Griffiths, L. Frampton, T. Richardson, F. Griffiths, G. Renouf, A. Pike, Mr Wilsden, T. Matthews. Front row: Mr Warne, Mr Gregory, Mr Perkins, A. Light, A. Cook, R. Richardson.

Shanklin C. of E. School football team, 1935, taken in the royal Silver Jubilee year. Back row, left to right: Mr Gent, -?-, John Burberry, 'Jigger' Holmes, Mr L.W. Downer. Middle row: John Slater, Ken Price, Sid Harding. Front row: 'Bunny' Hayden, Alan Brooks, Ken Dupre, Les Attrill, Boyton.

Shanklin Football Club youth team, 1949/50 season. Back row, left to right: Terry Shiner, Phil Attrill, Ralph Banting, Gus Long, Peter White, Joe Gueddes, Alf Gallop (Manager). Front row: Jeff Russell, Noel Gallop, Dave Orchard, Brian Bastiani, Derek Wells.

Shanklin Bowling Club Presidents' Day in jubilee year, 1978. Back row, left to right: Wilson Walker, George Sanderson, Stan Cook, Arthur Peacock, Jim Carter, Derek Webb, Joe Searles, John Nash, Ken Kimber, Richard Jefferey, Hilton Ridett, Alan Jefferey, Eric Maitland, Cyril Johnston, Hedley Guy, Will Russell, Gilbert Woodman, Ron Downer, Ken Hamblin, Rowley Swanborough, Bill Godfrey, Jack

Chapman, Ken Wakerely. Front row: Edith Godfrey, 'Pip' Bolton, Elsie Cade, Colin Ridett, Bernard Ridett, Steve Smart (Club President), Marjorie Brown, Harold Brown (President of the IOWCBA), Louis Wakerley, Vi Ridett, Joan Waterhouse, Molly Wyatt, Dorothy Russell, Jessie Millard, Betty Sanderson, Barbara Stiles.

Official opening of the Shanklin Bowling Green and Pavilion on Wednesday 4 May 1928. Among those attending were Alderman G. Mears, W. Blake, Mayor of Newport, Mr Green, H.W. Dawes, J.E.H. Terry, F. Parkinson, E. Dowling, C. Crawley, Percy Guy, H. Guy, Bob James, Ernest Cook, E. Cooper, Mr Mulliner, Ben Griffiths and J. Nichol.

Shanklin Football Club in 1895. This photograph was donated to the club by Mr J. Geddes, whose grandfather is third from the left, back row.

THE YOUTH

Mixed classes at Newchurch School, 1924. Included are Edwin Smith, Joe Hendy, Gordon Pointer, Barbara Taylor, Leslie Perkins, Ethel Brading, Ethel and Dorothy Buckett.

Sandown Cliff Rescue Service, 1951. Back row, left to right: A.E. Booth, W.J. Robinson, P. Farley, C.W. Dibbens, D. Pain, K.I. Hooper, R. Snow, W. Travers, E.G. Rapkins. Front row: G. Oatley, K.V. Brett, G. Moorman, C. Pardey.

Another picture of the Cliff Rescue Service showing a close-up of the standard equipment they carried, including the large rope ladder, stretcher, lifebelts and lamps. Pictured with their faithful Ford car are (left to right) W.J. Robinson, A.E. Booth and W. Travers.

The Sandown Cliff Rescue Service had its beginnings in the 1st Sandown Sea Scouts during the Second World War. During these early days much was learned about saving the lives of those who had fallen or were trapped on the cliff face. It fell to the Cliff Rescue Service to undertake many perilous missions and much is owed to those who gave their services so willingly. Pictured with their Ford motor car in 1951, the year they won the Scouts Silver Medal for gallantry, are (left to right) D. Pain, C.W. Dibbens, K.V. Brett and K.I. Hooper.

At the end of the nineteenth century, with the cessation of child labour, many customs involving the youth of our nation came into being. One such custom was 'shroving', which took place each Shrove Tuesday when confectionery was scattered for the children to catch and collect, a custom which unfortunately seems to have died out in modern times. Seen here in 1914 are the Newchurch village children.

Lord Baden-Powell talking to Prince Gustav of Sweden at a Scout rally in 1935. (Prince Gustav was later to die in an aeroplane accident.)

Grove Road School choir, 1951–2. Included are Georgiana Gladdis, Eileen Branton, Lyn Bounton, Brenda Dashwood, Eileen Abbott, Jill Mosdell, Cran Davies, Enid Chase, Jill Morgan, Sheila Jarman, Jill Maguire, Alan Maybey, Gary Grimes, Maureen Dowden, Marguerite Chase, Susan Moss, Daphne

Wheeler, Ann Paice, Janet Young, Maureen (Minnie) Toole, Sheila Dibbens, Maureen Taylor, June Driver, Janet Whittington, Jennifer Whitlock, Avril Gustar, Michael Hayward, Maureen O'Brien, 'Liz' Milton, Jennifer Pearson, Pam Tosdevin, Miss Wheeler and Mr Langford.

Miss McKenzie of Gatton and Lake School was well known for always wearing white gloves when she was teaching. Included here in her class of 1932 are Norman Smith, Betty Smith, Les Stratton, Brenda Forehead, Ken Phillips and Pearl Phillips.

The 1st Sandown Sea Scouts aboard a charabanc for a day trip, 1923 or 1924. Included are Thompson, Fuller, J. Herbert, Brown, Norris, Colenutt, Smith, Harris, V. Herbert and Ford.

The congregation of Apse Heath Chapel in 1905. Freida Gosden who attended the chapel has been identified by the placing of a black spot on her white hat.

Group 2 of Arreton National School, 1898. Unfortunately no names are available.

Class 1 of Arreton National School, 1906. Back row, left to right: Mr Jeatt, Robert Mackett, Walter James, George James, Percy Coombes, Reg Hiscock, Bert Galloway, George Mackett, Wilf Galloway. Third row: Daisy Whittington, Elsie Brown, Eva Hayward, Elsie James, 'Lottie' Brown, Ivy Whittington, Mrs Jeatt, Miss Scovell. Second row: Hilda Blake, Rosie Coombes, Kathy James, Lily James, Hedley Galloway, Walter Hiscock, William James, Henry James, Charles Whittington, Elsie Whittington, Dorothy Whittington. Front row: Gilbert Whittington, Arthur Brown, Sid Hiscock, Vic Hiscock, William Blake.

Group 3 of Arreton National School, 1895. Included are Ernest Galloway, Kathleen Jeatt, Mabel Smith, Elsie Russell, Millie Russell, Heilon Jeatt, William Jeatt, Elsie Edmonds, Clara Tutton, Arthur Orchard, Albert James, Henry Coombes, William Smith, Percy James, Gertie Burnett, Emily Orchard, Elizabeth Orchard, Frank Galloway, Charles Galloway, Douglas Jeatt, Miss Moore and Mr Jeatt.

Arreton National School, 1937. Shown here are Don Toney, Bob Coombes, Charlie Pitman, John Smith, Don Guy, Gordon Jones, Gladys Salter, Joan Smith, May Pragnell, Marion Butchers, Jill Ford, Rona Pragnell, Derek White, Herbert Long, Rosalie Francis, 'Cissie' Draper, Norah Galloway, Gwen Coombes, Jean Kennedy, Mona Cook, Florrie Brealey, Lily Guy, Harold Coombes, Roy Blake, Ian Kennedy, Raymond Cook, Ken Hobbs and Mr White.

AROUND THE TOWNS

*A common sight in the 1920s was a steamroller undertaking road repairs. One such roller is seen here in
St John's Road, Sandown.*

Shanklin Chine in 1894. The little girl in the photograph is believed to have been Eva Mitchell, who moved away from the island and at one point owned Shelley's Hotel in Lewis with her husband.

An old photograph taken from a glass-plate negative and showing the head of Shanklin Chine, 1880.

Shanklin Chine, 1909, with (left to right) Lawrence Hart, Sadie Hart, Olga Hart, Edne Hart and Eva Mitchell.

High Street, Sandown, 1910. On the extreme left are the offices of the *Isle of Wight Chronicle*, advertising their steam printers.

Carnegie Library, Sandown, 1928. The Jubilee Fountain is visible at the junction of the High Street and Avenue Road.

As the Isle of Wight opened up for the holiday-maker, so travel became available between the towns. As well as the small single horse and carriage type of conveyance, the coach and four were brought into being by firms such as Old Times. Here we see one ready for travel in 1890 outside the Old Times booking office situated at Merman's grocery store in Sandown.

Taylor's provision merchants of High Street, Sandown, 1901. The gentleman on the right of the picture may be Harry Brown, a member of the staff.

G. Butcher, the baker's shop in Avenue Road, Sandown, 1913. Jack Brett, Doris Really and Phoebie Nuckley are standing in the doorway..

The King's Head Hotel, Sandown, 1875.

Brown's ice cream factory in Sandown, 1939. During the Second World War this site took on a much more sinister purpose by housing the pumping station for PLUTO (Pipe Line Under The Ocean; see also p. 70).

Sandown Hotel, at the junction of Avenue Road and the High Street, *c.* 1880. At this time the main entrance to the hotel was in Avenue Road, rather than in Culver Parade as it is today.

Alverstone Mill continued to serve the public long after its closure. It is pictured here in 1932 as the Alverstone Mill Tea Gardens; it is interesting to note that cigarettes are included on the advertisement.

The White Lion Hotel and Vicarage Cottage, probably in 1933. It is here in St George's churchyard behind the White Lion, not far from the priest's door, that sunlight warms the headstone of the grave of Elizabeth Walbridge. Elizabeth was brought up in a cottage in Hale Common, placed into service at Knighton Gorges and died from consumption. Revd Leigh Richmond depicted her life in *The Dairyman's Daughter*.

Sandown Town Band outside the Oddfellows Hall, Station Avenue, 1890.

Sandown Town Band gave many concerts and won many contests. Here they are at the end of the pier
with their championship shield, probably in 1919.

Frank Moore at work in Downend brickyard, Arreton, 1930.

Arreton village in 1904. The two young ladies were daughters of the landlord of the White Lion.

Brooklyn, Holmleigh, Elim, Sunnyside and Laburnum cottages at Arreton, 1920. They were demolished in 1957 in the name of 'progress'.

The Chatsworth Boarding Establishment, Sandown, 1900. Later to become the Savoy Hotel, the building is now converted to separate flats.

Honeymoon Cottage, Shanklin Chine, 1908.

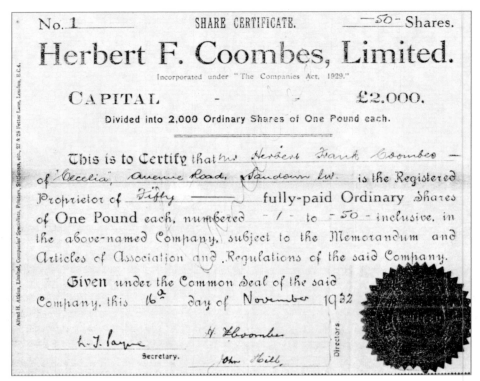

A copy of the share certificate for Herbert F. Coombes Ltd.

Sandown Operatic Society staged *A Sister to Visit* on 19 May 1915. In the centre of the front row is Captain Ellery of the Isle of Wight Rifles.

Rona and May Pragnell of Box Tree Cottage, Arreton, 1935. The cottage was destroyed by enemy aircraft in 1941.

The Sandown May Queen procession, 1946. The May Queen is 'Liz' Milton; also pictured are Bill Wyke (the small boy behind the Queen) and (at the rear) Graham Gustar and Terry Sears.

This view of Luccombe (date unknown) shows the gravel path which runs through the pleasant area of trees and shrubs to end up in the Luccombe Tea Garden.

Sandown firemen enjoying a well-earned rest from their duties outside Sandown Town Hall, *c.* 1907.

Guys' Corner Shop, Wilkes Road, Sandown. Standing by the shop front is 'Pop' Snow.

At the turn of the century many small shops were attached to the sides of the owner's residence. Here we see A.H. Butcher and his wife in 1902 with their lean-to shop selling everything from lamp oil to books.

Brading Bull Ring, 1926.

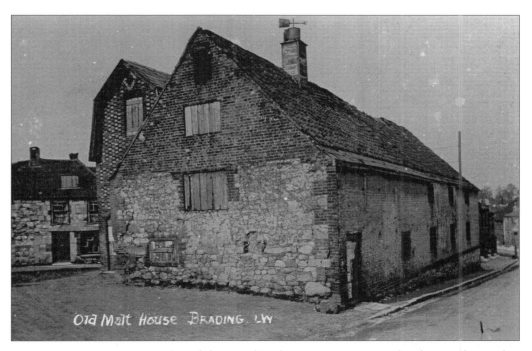

Most towns at one time possessed a malt house and Brading was no exception. This photograph was taken just before its demolition in 1893. In 1901 work commenced to build the new town hall on the site, which was completed in 1902 and opened by Princess Beatrice.

The chine at Shanklin has long been a must for visitors. During the Second World War the chine played a most important role, that of the English terminal of PLUTO (Pipe Line Under The Ocean), which was a long pipe laid under the sea to the Normandy beaches in order that fuel oil could be pumped to our troops on foreign soil. These four views of Shanklin Chine are spread over a period of twenty years: 1929 (top left), 1929 (top right), 1939 (bottom left) and 1949 (bottom right).

One of the resting places in Shanklin Chine built for the convenience of visitors, *c*. 1930.

Fisherman's Cottage, situated on the sea front at the base of Shanklin Chine. It was built in 1817 by Mr Colenutt, who was also the first to instigate the use of bathing machines in Shanklin, and it was owned by the family until the 1950s when Mrs Anne Springman, present owner of Shanklin Chine, purchased the lease. Until 1995 it was a club; it is now a successful free house.

The Old Village at Shanklin has always been a picturesque place. What is striking in this old photograph (date unknown) is the cleanliness and, of course, not a double yellow line in sight!

This view of Shanklin Old Village, taken in 1933 and made into a postcard, is often referred to as 'The Chocolate Box Card'.

A thatcher working at the Crab Hotel, Shanklin Old Village, 1930. The man standing in the entrance is Mr Marsh; the man nearest to the camera lounging against the fence is Percy Saunders. It is unfortunate that thatching is no longer the main roofing on the island, but in common with many areas in Dorset and the West of England many thatched cottages remain here and add to the beauty of the small villages.

The landlord and his wife, George and Audrey Moore, at the Crab Hotel, Shanklin Old Village, when they took over from George's father on his retirement in the 1950s. Mr Moore senior had been the landlord since 1946.

Inside the Crab Hotel in 1959, just after the changeover. Pictured (left to right) are Maureen James, Gladys Bunn, George Bunn and Patrick Jefferies.

In 1906, the Crab Hotel was also known as the Old Inn. The man in the doorway is Mr Spenser, grandson of the landlord. Beside him is the white tablecloth covering the table on which they kept freshly made lemonade.

An early photograph of Ryalstone House. It is now the setting for Ryalstone Gardens, a public park situated off Popham Road.

Old Park Cottage, Arreton, in 1901 (above). The baby in the pram is Linda Butcher, with Rosina Butcher standing by the hedge. Linda and Rosina lived at the cottage until its demolition in 1958. On the site was built a row of bungalows known as Park Cottages (below). The two sisters took up residence there.

In common with many other small island villages, many fayres and fêtes have been held in Newchurch, but none so popular as the annual Queen of Beauty Pageant founded by Revd J.M. Banford at the start of this century. Many leading island dignataries of the day regarded it as an honour to be asked to attend. Much merriment would take place before the actual crowning of the Queen. Pictured here is maypole dancing at the fête held on 3 August 1908.

The MP for the Island, Douglas Hall, pictured with the Headmaster of Newchurch School, Mr 'Skipper' Clark, at the Queen of Beauty Pageant at Newchurch in 1912.

From the tea rooms and bustle of Shanklin village you clamber down a damp contorted rift aptly called the Devil's Chimney into the tangle of planted and tumbled terrain of The Landslip. Here is a stone seat on which to sit while contemplating that fateful night in 1810 when 25 acres of land on blue slipper plunged to sea level. Blue slipper is a form of soft rock on fine sand which crumbles when drying after heavy rain

Keat's Green, Shanklin, in the 1950s.

The island has little in the way of inland waterways, but on the River Yar at Alverstone boating was a common pastime. This photograph was taken in 1932.

Their names are no longer known by many of us but their deeds will never be forgotten. In the dark days of the last war, the men of Shanklin did not hesitate to come forward to serve their country in the armed services and home guard.

Newchurch railway station, *c.* 1904. The station master is awaiting a train to Sandown.

This thatched cottage at Newchurch, called Princelett, was used as a canteen for German troops stationed here in the 1800s during the Napoleonic Wars. The German regiment in question was the Lowenstein Hasseurs, Kodenz Regt.

Apse Heath boasted their own baker and confectioner, C.M. Taylor & Sons Ltd. They won many awards in the 1940s for their high quality produce.

The ladies and gentlemen of Newchurch would turn out in force to watch the hunt go by. Here we see the hunt approaching the village in 1906.

The Newchurch Hunt as they set out on the downs above the village, 1930.

In the early years of this century a group of threshers with their steam-driven engine would move from farm to farm during the harvest season. Fred Corny and Nathan Smith, among others, are pictured above. The lower photograph shows some of the threshing crew at Winford at the end of the day's toil, with the worker on the left preparing the lamp to leave by the machine.

Apse Heath brickyard in 1932, at a time when bricks were made by hand. The brickmakers are F. Peach and J. Whittington; their pugboys are W. Hutching and G. Bettenson. (A pugboy prepares the clay ready for the brickmaker.)

William Thatcher with his wife and daughter at the entrance to Wackland, 1868. William was a breeder of champion fighting cocks and as his fame spread it led to the naming of Fighting Cocks Cross and the Fighting Cocks public house. Wackland was built in 1736 and set between lakes with a viewing tower over an arena in which the cock fights took place.

TRANSPORT

Ted Hudges taking schoolgirls on a trip around the island, at Daish's Corner in Shanklin, 1920s.

Victoria Avenue, Shanklin, on 24 September 1919, when the female staff of Grays set out on a trip to Alum Bay and Totland.

Bembridge station, 1930. The station will be remembered by the thousands of young people who camped with the many youth groups using Whitecliffe Bay as their main centre. Alighting from the train at Bembridge they would walk along the footpaths to reach the bay.

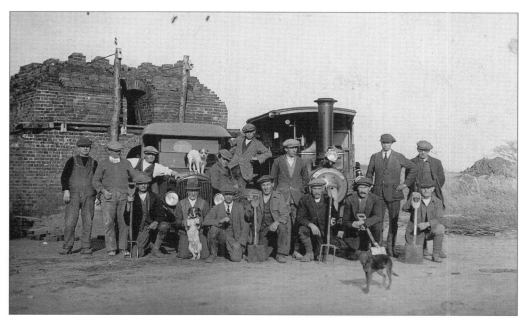

Downend brickyard in 1925. Back row, left to right: D. Taylor, A. Taylor, S. Newland, L. James, H. Gallop with 'Beaver' the dog, R. Dore (on lorry), H. Hemmings, W. Mowbray. Front row: Joe Whittington, F. Moore with 'Chum' the dog, M. Moore, Charlie Butcher, Sam Knapp, Albert Hendy, William Smith and 'Dusky' the dog.

With the housing boom of 1936, Downend brickyard was never busier. Claud Mowbray and Martin Moore are on the lorry; William Smith and Albert Young (facing camera) are loading bricks.

The Downend Brick and Tar Company lorry on Arreton Down in 1921 (above). Just after 1935 the company changed its name to the Downend Brick Manufacturing Company. Pictured below after this change are, back row, left to right: Martin Moore (in lorry), Albert Young, William Smith and William Mowbray Jnr. Middle row: Frank Moore (sitting on lorry). Front row: Steve Newland, Claud Mowbray, Charlie Cole and Leslie Cole.

A familiar figure in 1910 was Miss M. Read, who was often to be seen driving her pony and trap between Sandown and Newchurch.

A coach and four about to depart from the Stag Inn at Lake in the early 1900s. One of the ladies is believed to be Emily Swinbourne, who was visiting her mother in Shanklin.

Eames Garage of Sandown, one of the early pioneers of motor coach and charabanc travel. This photograph, taken in the late 1920s, shows waiting buses and staff receiving their orders for the day. The company vacated the garage in the early 1960s and it was taken over by Hodge and Childs.

One of the early buses, DL 6829, making its way along the toll road at Seaview.

Walkden's Garage, Avenue Road, Sandown, where coaches with their drivers are waiting to start work. Pictured here in the early 1930s are (left to right) George Cash, Alf White, Alec Crocker, Ken Tosdevin, Bert Southcott, Walt Warne, -?-, Roly Ramsden, Sid Masters, Ray Warder, Reg Selwood and -?-.

Shanklin bus station, built in the 1950s, became the main home of public transport on the eastern side of the island. It's a pity it was not built with Downend bricks instead of the drab London brick.

The building of a bus station cannot be allowed to stop the flow of buses. The Shanklin bus station featured in these two photographs was built in the early 1950s and served the town until its demolition in 1983.

Little has changed since this photograph was taken in the 1950s: Shanklin High Street at this point is still as hazardous.

A great favourite with holiday-makers in fine weather is to ride on the top deck of an open-top bus from Ryalstone Gardens and around the town of Shanklin. This photograph was taken in 1970.

An open-top bus in the mid-1960s passing Newport Road, Lake. This point in the road is known locally as Threeways Corner but referred to colloquially by many of the bus crews as 'Take Away Corner' because of the lovely fish and chips which were sold at the start of Newport Road.

In the 1920s no self-respecting holiday-maker would visit the seaside without taking a trip around the bay. Seen here is one of Blake's launches returning to Sandown beach, 14 July 1927.

BESIDE THE SEASIDE

Keat's Green and East Cliff Promenade, Shanklin, in the 1950s.

The Western Esplanade, Sandown, from a postcard sent to Arreton in 1912.

Shanklin Esplanade looked entirely different in 1919.

This view of Fisherman's Cottage at the bottom of Shanklin Chine, 1933, clearly shows the initiative of the owners, with canoes lined up catering for the holiday-maker.

Sandown beach in the 1920s, showing the portable boarding gangplank for small pleasure boats.

Traversing the footpath from Sandown to Bembridge one has to climb over Culver Cliff. This 1911 photograph shows the start of the path where it passed a high stand of corn less than 50 yards from the high tide line.

This view of Shanklin pier and sea front is believed to have been taken between 1920 and 1922. Notice the bathing huts being towed into the water.

Luccombe Chine in 1950. This well-known beauty spot is worth the descent of the 235 steps it takes to reach the beach. It is now completely wild and unspoilt; even the fishermen's cottages which once graced the lower slopes have disappeared. It was here in 1946 that the bones of a gigantic sauropod were found on the beach, so it pays to be observant!

Shanklin sea front in 1878, showing the area on which the pier was later built. This structure, completed in 1891, which has over the years afforded so much pleasure to so many, fell short of celebrating its centenary by four years. Tragically, it was destroyed overnight during the hurricanes of October 1987.

Pier Street, Sandown, 1919.

The beach at Shanklin in 1905, before the construction of the holiday amenities which make it the Shanklin we know today.

At the turn of the century the Esplanade at Sandown was beginning to look something akin to how we know it today. Here we see the bottom of Avenue Slipway in 1900.

After the cessation of hostilities in 1918, many new attractions were opened on the Western Esplanade at Sandown. These included the Parade Kinema, situated beyond Vectis Hall.

Taken in the early 1950s, this photograph of Luccombe Common again shows the wild desolation of the area.

Shanklin beach, 1892. In the early days of sea bathing, males and females would bathe on different days on separate beaches and never the twain would meet, but the advent of mixed bathing saw the use of the bathing machine for changing. These would be wheeled down to the water's edge, thus allowing the bather to change inside them and step down into the sea.

With the coming of street lighting, promenading along the Western Esplanade in Sandown was more accessible to evening strollers.

This photograph of Shanklin beach and sea front, taken from the pier in 1936, shows the many rowing boats which were for hire.

Sandown Esplanade in 1908, which bears little resemblance to the hustle and bustle of today's seaside resort.

This view of Shanklin was taken in 1952 from the pathway to Luccombe Common on the site of the Old Priory.

A small cluster of buildings on Sandown beach at the southern end of the town, probably just before the First World War.

Small Hope beach, Shanklin, was popular for bathing in the 1930s. What a wealth of motoring history is featured in this photograph.

In the spring of 1878 Sir Winston Churchill, then a young boy of four, was to witness one of the worst disasters in the annals of seafaring. Many decades later, Sir Winston recorded in his memoirs, *My Early Life*, that the stories of divers finding corpses half eaten away by fish left scars on his mind. The ship involved was the 920 ton HMS *Eurydice*. Carrying four guns, she was homeward bound from Bermuda and crammed with troops looking forward to leave. When *Eurydice* left the shelter of the high cliffs around Dunnose Point, Shanklin, she was enveloped in a freak snowstorm so fierce that she sank almost immediately with the loss of over 300 lives. Later, she was salvaged and beached, as seen in this photograph taken from an old glass-plate negative.

The Hooper family, longshoremen, posing in front of a Sandown bathing machine in 1892.

A photograph taken in 1875 of the Ocean View Hotel, Sandown, and adjacent area.

Sandown pictured from the pier in 1908. It is interesting to see the clothes hanging on lines along the sea wall (far left).

The Western Esplanade in 1908, as seen from the pier entrance.

The Western Esplanade, Sandown, looking east towards the pier, 1890.

A popular hotel in 1890 was the King's Head, Sandown.

Vectis Hall, after extensive additions in 1925. To the south the tower of the Parade Kinema can just be seen. In that year the high spring tides left an unusual amount of shingle on this normally sandy beach.

Crowds gathering to enjoy a performance by the band in Guadeloupe Terrace, Sandown, 1912.

The bathing beach at Sandown, looking south towards Shanklin, 1906.

Girls will be girls, even on Sandown beach in the 1920s. Here are seven of them showing off the latest fashions in swimwear.

Shanklin Pier entrance in 1900.

The Old Arcade on the Western Esplanade, Sandown, 1890.

Guadeloupe Terrace, one of the most grandiose and yet controversial edifices ever constructed in Sandown and later to be converted into hotels.

One of the oldest photographs in the book, from a glass-plate negative taken in 1869. It shows the view looking south from the grounds of the King's Head Hotel. Guadeloupe Terrace had then not been built and the gardens reached down to the sea wall. Many of the boats were owned by the hotel and used by its guests.

Sandown had its own small fishing village on the beach just south of the town. Leaning against his boat on 26 April 1906 is Mr H.K. Richardson with Willie.

PLACES OF WORSHIP

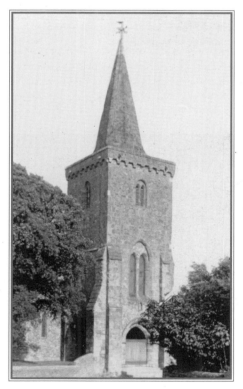

*The twelfth-century parish church of St Mary,
Brading, now supports a tower containing eight
bells, dating from 1594 onwards. Among its niches,
lancets and Purbeck marble pilasters are many
memorials. This picture was taken in 1904.*

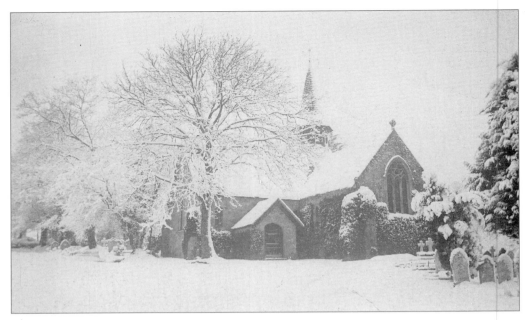

St Blazius, Shanklin Old Church in the snow of 1909.

The fifteenth-century Oglander Chapel in the church of St Mary, Brading. Oak effigies of Sir William and Sir John Oglander were placed there on instructions of the latter's will, sturdily reclining upon tomb-chests; their rolled campaign mats, armour and Crusader postures are anachronistic.

The accommodation block (above) and chapel (below) of the Girls' Friendly Society Hostel and Home of Rest at Shanklin, 1951.

Members of Sandown Baptist Church on an outing in 1901.

The Methodist Chapel at Arreton, built in 1866 and pictured in 1905, has changed little to this day.

THE PIERS

Beach entertainment has always been popular. This photograph was taken on Sandown beach in 1897.

By 1910, two small shelters had been added halfway along the length of Sandown Pier, thus affording some protection against the inclement and sudden changes in the weather that promenaders had to endure.

Shanklin Pier in 1903, with an entirely different sea front to the one we know today.

The opening of the extended Sandown Pier in 1895.

A pierrot show on the sea front at Sandown, 1900. Pierrot shows were just one of a number of entertainments staged on the Esplanade at this time.

A view of Sandown Pier from the southern cliffs, 1890.

The Parade Kinema on the Western Esplanade, Sandown, 1920.

As we can see from this photograph, taken in 1900, piers were originally constructed mainly for promenading. Little was available in the way of the amusements we would expect today.

As Sandown became more popular with holiday-makers, it was decided to extend the pier. Work was completed in 1895. The pierhead pavilion can just be seen in this photograph.

The original entrance to Sandown Pier, 1879.

This unusual view of Shanklin beach was taken when bathing machines were in vogue, but no precise date is known.

The beach and pier, Sandown, 1920. Once again, notice the abundance of bathing machines to protect the modesty of those wishing to bathe.

ACKNOWLEDGEMENTS

This book would not have been possible but for the assistance given by so many people. I would therefore like to thank the following: Ron and Rose Chase of Cowplain, Hants.; R. Downer; Bert Draper; J. Gould; 'Chick' Hickling; Councillor Heather Humby; Dr Alan Insole; Malcolm Johnson; J. Lavers; C. Leal; Audrey Moore; M. Nicholson; Bill Patten; Ken Phillips; Wayne Pritchett, Harbour Master, Newport Quay; E.G. (Ewart) Rapkins; Sandown and Shanklin Golf Club; Shanklin Bowling Club; Shanklin Football Club; and A. Thatcher.

I would especially like to acknowledge the help given in the preparation of this book by the following people and associations: John Howell and Trudy Price, Sandown Historical Association; Terry Hall, Archivist, Sandown Civic Centre; Simon Dabell, Director of Blackgang Chine Theme Park; Anne Springman, Shanklin Chine and Fisherman's Cottage; and Peter T.G. White.